#LiveIntentionally
4
STUDENTS
26-Week Challenge

by
Mark D. Bush

In loving memory of my
Mother, Chandlyn Anthony

Table of Contents

Preface

"Remember whose name you have," my pops, Corby Bush Sr. would tell us before leaving the house, growing up. I knew exactly what he meant; I represent my family in everything I do, good or bad. Here's the thing, my last name was not always Bush, I was born Mark Anthony. When I think about proud moments, I can't help but to think about how proud I was to become a Bush.

I was born to the beautiful Chicagoan, Chandlyn Anthony and her husband Randy Anthony. I came in this world with my twin brother, affectionately known as my "wombmate", Marlon Anthony November 22, 1982. My parents separated after my mother filed a battery complaint against Randy, after a series of arguments had turned into violent fights. March 23, 1986, two weeks after my parents had separated; Marlon and I were in the kitchen with our mother as she washed dishes. On that Sunday morning, we heard the crashing sound of our front door slamming against the wall as it was furiously opened, it was Randy. Their argument echoed throughout the entire house. The arguing turned into a violent fight ending with Randy stabbing mother. My mother fell to the kitchen floor lifeless. My brother and I were three years old, witnessed the entire incident and understood everything that had happened. Mother was gone.

Randy left or house and drove to the train station on Pulaski Road and Lake Street. He stood on the edge of the train platform where he removed his wallet and set it down next to himself. As onlookers watched, Randy warned them to stay back. He yelled, "Tell my mother I'm sorry," before jumping in front of an arriving train. This day forever changed my life.

My uncle, Corby Bush didn't hesitate. He adopted my twin brother and I as well as our eldest sibling, Jason who is three years older than us.

Corby Bush, 24 years old, was married to Yvonne Bush of Maywood, IL and father of Kristen Bush, who was one years old at the time. I am now33 years old and still can't imagine the enormous amount of responsibility thrust upon him.

For the longest, I referred to my mother's brother as Uncle Corby. Even though he was my adoptive father, I was still his nephew. I never felt unloved or unequally loved as his child. However, I felt embarrassed when people would ask about my last name, why wasn't it the same? I remember the way members of our church made us feel. They made us feel like we were inferior to our cousins, they didn't treat us the same. I felt people made a fuss over and loved them more and we were the extra baggage.

When I was younger, I felt ashamed that I didn't have a mom or dad of my own. As the years passed, that feeling changed drastically. The dynamic of our family changed, as well. We were no longer nephews and cousins; we were sons, brothers and sisters. My uncle wouldn't respond unless we called him, "father". We had to consciously be trained to call my uncle "father". I remember people used to mock us because we called him father, it sounded too proper for some. I was proud to call him father, and from then on he was just that.

It was the summer before we were to start high school; my father was keeping a surprise. He was changing our last name to Bush, my mother's maiden name, but more importantly, his name. Changing our last name wasn't the surprise; he was giving us a middle name and wouldn't tell us until our court date. Giving us our middle names was his way of being able to name *his* sons. The anticipation was killing me. I had always wanted a middle name, and I had no idea what it would be. On (enter date here), I went from Mark Anthony to Mark Devin Bush. You know how some people hate their middle name or don't want people to know what it is. Not me; I was incredibly proud of mine. I think I would have been proud if my middle name was Stellan. It wasn't about the name; it was about the man who gave it to me. I was now a Bush, and like my father used to tell us, "Remember who you represent." I represented the Bush family name.

It wasn't until I started writing this book, that I ever asked my father why he named me Devin. He told me that Devin meant, "Victorious leader and strong will". He went on to say, "it means harmony or poet, like a person who knows how to bring things together. That's why it came to mean "victorious leader and strong will."

I can remember the countless conversations my father and I had as a child. I would sit on the closed toilet lid in his bathroom and listen to him talk, while he shaved. While talking, he would make eye contact with me after every stroke of his butter knife against his thick beard. He would ask, "Mark, you understand what I'm saying?" My father would talk to me about the only things a man has, his name and his integrity. One day when I was about eleven or twelve, my father was talking to me. As I sit here and write, I can vividly remember how proud I was of the man my father was. At this point in my life, my father was 31, raising eight children (me and my two brothers, four children of his own, and his other two nephews), founded his first church in Oak Park, IL, while attending Moody Bible Institute for his undergraduate degree. My father was definitely someone to admire. I looked up at him and told him, "Father, I want to be just like you when I grow up." I have never forgotten his words, something that drives me today, "Son, I want you to be better than me." "Son, I want you to be better than me." There are times in my life; I honestly do not have any idea of how this would even have been possible. My father is a world-renowned, well sought after, Pentecostal Bishop with the Church of God In Christ, Inc. Here's the thing, we will never know if we don't try.

When I was younger, I still silently struggled with the loss of my mother. There was a point I didn't understand why I had to lose MY mother. I didn't have a chance to have memories of her scent, her voice, her touch, or what she looked like without a picture. I felt robbed. My father was preaching one Sunday. He said something that changed my life, "Everything happens for a reason, God has a purpose for everything He does." It changed my outlook on my situation: I was not a victim; I was a victor.

I never knew what kept Randy from taking the lives of my brother and me; we were in the same room. I was not a victim; God spared my life because I had a purpose to fulfill. My purpose was to live intentionally. Live with a sense of purpose. Intentionally impact everything I do and every person I come across. I occasionally receive messages asking how I keep a positive upbeat outlook on life. I want to pass on the blessing that arose from tragedy. I want to share to inspire and uplift as many people as possible. Isn't that what life's about? Impact…Impacting the people around us and everything we touch. It has to be a conscious and intentional decision. Change your mindset…you'll change your life, you'll impact lives.

In my initial brainstorming phase of #LiveIntentionally, I started compiling stories of the impact my life has had on others by living intentionally. I felt a reader could be taken back by the style of telling my story. I want to avoid this being viewed as a pretentious, "look at me" story. I stopped writing and began thinking of how I could get my point across to any reader; those who know me and those who do not.

#LiveIntentionally hit me while driving through downtown Atlanta. Creating an experience of #LiveIntentionally as opposed to assimilating through reading was a far greater lesson. If my intentions were to impact your lives, you'd need to *feel* an intentional life, not read about it.

Introduction

The idea of this challenge came to me after several conversations with a childhood friend of mine, Marcia Collins. Marcia and I talk often about the things we're up to and have kept in touch for a little over 18 years. Marcia, along with a few other friends of mine who have followed me on social media, often see my many post and pictures of what I'm up to and what I'm working on. They usually send me text messages asking what is it that I do that keeps me motivated and positive. I simply reply, "I focus on others." Which is usually followed by the question, "How?"

I usually share with them how I intentionally take my focus off of me and what may be bothering me. This is not to be confused with ignoring my problems. I don't sulk or as my mother would say, "have a pity party", for myself. I usually do two

1

things to cope with negativity and depression. First, I draw attention away from myself and reflect on the things my family, friends, or co-workers may be dealing with. Then, I intentionally "make someone's day". Nothing crazy, I do intentional acts of kindness- random act for the individual receiving the kindness, but very much so calculated on my end. This LIFE CHANGING journal invites you to love intentionally, through my Reflection Sundays and "Intentional Acts of Kindness"...not random acts of kindness, there was nothing random about it.

REFLECTION SUNDAYS

Reflection Sundays is something I came up with a while ago. A few years ago, I found myself at what I thought, at the time, was the hardest time of my life. I kept falling into a deep depression; I refused to see the light at the end of the tunnel. Like most, I struggled alone...I didn't want to appear "weak".

I could hear my mom in the back of my head, "there's no time for pity parties". I remember I picked up a pen and note pad, I began writing:

>*Joey Oberndorfer –Police Academy grad Oct 15*
>*Faris Flournoy – Primecare Home Care growth*
>*Nathan Hawkins – Assignment and SOS School*

Father – Healthy Recovery
Riley Gill – Body Building Competition May 23
Josh O. – Birth of his son Elijah Jeremiah due Aug
Aaron Marquez – Dog Lobo surgery May 27
Jamie Romo – Nursing School
Brian Creswell – Loss mother June 3

Every Sunday, I would come to this list to pray for, think about, and communicate with the individuals on the list. I would send a text or call the people on my list to encourage, check up, and listen to the person on the other side of my phone. It was all about them, I was just there for them.

THE CHALLENGE

Over the course of the next 26-weeks, I challenge you to take my weekly "Intentional Acts of Kindness" and brighten someone's day. The challenges will give you ideas for things to do for your family, friends, co-workers, employees, employers, neighbors. However, there's a twist. Some challenges will force you to step out of your comfort zone. Each challenge has three levels. You can choose the level of which you can accomplish. It is a challenge, each week do more than you think you can – Challenge yourself!

Once your challenge is complete, you can "log" your experience, and intentionally use the "hashtag" provided in your social media post the day you complete your challenge. Every fourth week will consist of the same challenge, "Meet a New Student". You will be challenged to talk to a student you've never talked to before or student you may know nothing about. Use this challenge to find out their "story" and how you can be a friend to them.

Lastly, you will be responsible for creating and maintaining your "Reflection Sunday" list, every week. The concept of this challenge is to intentionally change your behavior. We change our behavior, we change the world!

Join our *closed* Facebook community to share your experiences during this challenge:
www.facebook.com/groups/LiveIntentionally

Follow Me:
Twitter: @MrBeIntentional
Periscope: @MrBeIntentional
Facebook: www.facebook.com/MrBeIntentional

1. Faris Flournoy – Primecare Home Care

2.

3.

#ReflectionSunday

Join our closed Facebook community to share your experiences during this challenge:
www.facebook.com/groups/LiveIntentionally

#ReflectionSunday

Join our closed Facebook community to share your experiences during this challenge:
www.facebook.com/groups/LiveIntentionally

#Reflection Sunday

Join our closed Facebook community to share your experiences during this challenge:
www.facebook.com/groups/LiveIntentionally

#ReflectionSunday

Join our closed Facebook community to share your experiences during this challenge:
www.facebook.com/groups/LiveIntentionally

#Reflection Sunday

Join our closed Facebook community to share your experiences during this challenge:
www.facebook.com/groups/LiveIntentionally

#ReflectionSunday

Join our closed Facebook community to share your experiences during this challenge:
www.facebook.com/groups/LiveIntentionally

#Reflection Sunday

Join our closed Facebook community to share your experiences during this challenge:
www.facebook.com/groups/LiveIntentionally

#ReflectionSunday

Join our closed Facebook community to share your experiences during this challenge:
www.facebook.com/groups/LiveIntentionally

#Reflection Sunday

Join our closed Facebook community to share your experiences during this challenge:
www.facebook.com/groups/LiveIntentionally

<u>Week 1</u>

Intentionally Wake Up

Level 1,2, & 3 - Each day this week. Wake up the first time your parents/guardians or alarm clock goes off. Count to 3, once you get to 3 your feet have to hit the ground and you have to start your day!

#ItsANewDay
#LiveIntentionally

Recipient of your Challenge:

Recipient's Reaction:

How did it make you feel?

Week 2

Intentionally Eat

Level 1 - Each day this week, assist someone with cleaning their area after lunch

Level 2 & 3 - One day this week, sit at a new table or with a new group. Introduce yourself and learn something interesting about that group.

#LunchWasInteresting
#LiveIntentionally

Recipient of your Challenge:

Recipient's Reaction:

How did it make you feel?

Week 3

Intentionally Thank A Building Custodian
(Actions Speaks Louder than Words...we'll do both)

Level 1 - When you get to school this week, pick up any trash you see inside of the building.

Level 2 - After School 1 day this week, grab a friend and spend 15 mins picking up the trash around your building.

Level 3 - Each day this week, spend 30 mins picking up trash inside or outside your school. At the end of your challenge, leave a message of thanks for the building custodian with a teacher or front office.

#KeepingItClean
#LiveIntentionally

Recipient of your Challenge:

Recipient's Reaction:

How did it make you feel?

Week 4

Intentionally Meet a New Student Challenge

Level 1 - Introduce yourself to a student you've never met before in your school.

Level 2 - Invite a student you've never talked to before to hang out with you and your friends

Level 3 - Meet 2 students you've never talked to before, invite the student to hang with you and your friends 3 days of this week, and find out 4 things you all have in common.

#NewFriend
#LiveIntentionally

Recipient of your Challenge:

Recipient's Reaction:

How did it make you feel?

Week 5

Intentionally Help the Elderly Challenge

Level 1 - Call your grandparents twice this week to talk to them

Level 2 - Go to your local grocery store and help ALL elderly customers for an hour.

Level 3 - Pick a day this week to go by a Nursing Home in your community and volunteer.

#ILoveSeniors
#LiveIntentionally

Recipient of your Challenge:

Recipient's Reaction:

How did it make you feel?

Week 6

Intentionally Appreciate Your Siblings

Level 1, 2, & 3 - Think about 5 things you love about each of your siblings. Monday - Friday, write down one thing at a time, leave it somewhere they'd find it each day this week. If you don't have a sibling, do the challenge for your best friend.

#Fam
#LiveIntentionally

Recipient of your Challenge:

Recipient's Reaction:

How did it make you feel?

Week 7

Intentionally Volunteer Challenge

Level 1 - Ask your parents/guardians for an extra chore this week...with a smile and no added allowance.

Level 2 - Ask your parents for a challenging task that might take a few days to complete and OWN IT!

Level 3 - Find a place you can volunteer and dedicate some time to helping out. (thrift store, hospital, nursing home, etc)

#IGotThis
#LiveIntentionally

Recipient of your Challenge:

Recipient's Reaction:

How did it make you feel?

Week 8

Intentionally Meet a New Student Challenge

Level 1 - Introduce yourself to a student you've never met before in your school.

Level 2 - Invite a student you've never talked to before to hang out with you and your friends

Level 3 - Meet 2 students you've never talked to before, invite the student to hang with you and your friends 3 days of this week, and find out 4 things you all have in common.

#NewFriend
#LiveIntentionally

Recipient of your Challenge:

Recipient's Reaction:

How did it make you feel?

Week 9

Intentionally Appreciate a Teacher

Level 1 - Tell your teacher(s) 4 things you like about them.

Level 2 - Write a message to your teacher(s) and let them know they're doing a great job.

Level 3 - Think about 1 or 2 teachers (past or present) who's had the biggest impact in your life. Write a letter letting them know the impact they've had on your life and give it to them.

#TeachersAreAwesome
#LiveIntentionally

Recipient of your Challenge:

Recipient's Reaction:

How did it make you feel?

Week 10

Intentionally Keep Up

Level 1 - Ask your parent/guardian/teacher for information on a current news event. Discuss and journal what you learned.

Level 2 & 3 - Find a local news article, journal what you learned, have a random discussion about it with your peers and see what they think.

#WhatsUp
#LiveIntentionally

Recipient of your Challenge:

Recipient's Reaction:

How did it make you feel?

Week 11
Intentionally Positive

Level 1 - This week, every time you see someone you know for the first time in that day, give a high-five and say something that will put a smile on their face i.e., joke, encouraging words, etc.

Level 2 - Starting on Monday, go one full day without complaining. Intentionally stop yourself if you're about to complain. If you complain, your challenge starts over the next day. Keep a tally of how many times you complained or stopped yourself from complaining and log it in your journaling for this challenge.

Level 3 - Each Day this week, find a different motivational quote and share it with someone you think needs it. Starting on Monday, go one full day without complaining. Intentionally stop yourself if you're about to complain. If you complain, your challenge starts over the next day. Keep a tally of how many times you complained or stopped yourself from complaining and log it in your journaling for this challenge.

#StayPositive

Recipient of your Challenge:

Recipient's Reaction:

How did it make you feel?

Week 12

Intentionally Meet a New Student Challenge

Level 1 - Introduce yourself to a student you've never met before in your school.

Level 2 - Invite a student you've never talked to before to hangout with you and your friends

Level 3 - Meet 2 students you've never talked to before, invite the student to hang with you and your friends 3 days of this week, and find out 4 things you all have in common.

#NewFriend
#LiveIntentionally

Recipient of your Challenge:

Recipient's Reaction:

How did it make you feel?

Week 13

CONGRATULATIONS!!!

You are half way through your challenge. Use this week to reflect on the impact your life has had on others through INTENTIOANLLY seeking people out to brighten their day. Your intentional acts of kindness have gone a long way. Take a few notes about how you feel.

#IntentionallyReflect

Twitter: @MrBeIntentional
Periscope: @MrBeIntentional
Facebook: www.facebook.com/MrBeIntentional

Recipient of your Challenge:

Recipient's Reaction:

How did it make you feel?

Week 14

Intentionally Appreciate The Office Staff

Level 1 - Stop by the main office and thank them for what they do.

Level 2 & 3 - During your lunch break, write a small message to thank the office staff for what they do. Stop by and drop it off for them to read when you leave.

#TheyWorkHard
#LiveIntentionally

Recipient of your Challenge:

Recipient's Reaction:

How did it make you feel?

Week 15

Intentionally Try A NEW Hobby

Level 1 - Ask your parents/guardians about their hobbies, do it with them.

Level 2 & 3 - Ask a friend about a *good* hobby you don't have in common. Spend this week doing it with them and see what you think.

#NewHobby
#LiveIntentionally

Recipient of your Challenge:

Recipient's Reaction:

How did it make you feel?

Week 16

Intentionally Meet a New Student Challenge

Level 1 - Introduce yourself to a student you've never met before in your school.

Level 2 - Invite a student you've never talked to before to hangout with you and your friends

Level 3 - Meet 2 students you've never talked to before, invite the student to hang with you and your friends 3 days of this week, and find out 4 things you all have in common.

#NewFriend
#LiveIntentionally

Recipient of your Challenge:

Recipient's Reaction:

How did it make you feel?

Week 17

Intentionally Appreciate a Cop

Level 1 - As you pass the Crossing Guard this morning, say, "Thank you for keeping us safe."

Level 2 - Write a small message of thanks to a police officer. If you see one this week, give it to them. If you don't, ask your parents/guardian if you can stop by the police station to give it to them personally.

Level 3 - Use this week to get to know something about a local police officer and why they do what they do. Thank them for what they do and let them know you're grateful for their sacrifice.

#ThankACop
#LiveIntentionally

Recipient of your Challenge:

Recipient's Reaction:

How did it make you feel?

Week 18

Intentionally Like Your Least Favorite Student

Level 1 - For an entire day this week, only say nice things to your least favorite student in class.

Level 2 - Let your least favorite student know 5 things you like about them... see if you all have anything in common, while you're at it.

Level 3 - Find your least favorite student and learn "their story". Everyone has a story, you learn their story, you'll learn how to be a friend to them. TRY IT!

#NotSoBad.
#LiveIntentionally

Recipient of your Challenge:

Recipient's Reaction:

How did it make you feel?

Week 19

Intentionally Help A Student

Level 1 - Help another student with class work or homework, every day this week.

Level 2 - Ask a teacher in a lower grade if you can assist in their class, one day this week.

Level 3 - Think about your best subject, ask the teacher of that subject if anyone needs tutoring. Spend this week tutoring someone.

#ICanTeach
#LiveIntentionally

Recipient of your Challenge:

Recipient's Reaction:

How did it make you feel?

Week 20

Intentionally Meet a New Student Challenge

Level 1 - Introduce yourself to a student you've never met before in your school.

Level 2 - Invite a student you've never talked to before to hangout with you and your friends

Level 3 - Meet 2 students you've never talked to before, invite the student to hang with you and your friends 3 days of this week, and find out 4 things you all have in common.

#NewFriend
#LiveIntentionally

Recipient of your Challenge:

Recipient's Reaction:

How did it make you feel?

<u>Week 21</u>

Intentionally Eat

Level 1 - Each day this week, assist someone with cleaning their area after lunch

Level 2 & 3 - Two days this week, sit at a new table or with a new group. Introduce yourself and learn something interesting about that group.

#LunchWasInteresting
#LiveIntentionally

Recipient of your Challenge:

Recipient's Reaction:

How did it make you feel?

Week 22

Intentionally Give

Level 1, 2, & 3 - Use this week to intentionally pack up old items of clothes, toys, etc. Donate to a family who could use it or donate to a thrift store in your community.

#BKind
#LiveIntentionally

Recipient of your Challenge:

Recipient's Reaction:

How did it make you feel?

Week 23

Intentionally Appreciate the Principal

Level 1 - Think of 2 things you like about your principle, write a short message that includes those things. Fold the message and write "For the Principle" on it, leave it at the main office.

Level 1 - Think of 4 things you like about your principle, write a short message that includes those things. Fold the message and write "For the Principle" on it, leave it at the main office.

#MyPrincipalIsCool
#LiveIntentionally

Recipient of your Challenge:

Recipient's Reaction:

How did it make you feel?

Week 24

Intentionally Meet a New Student Challenge

Level 1 - Introduce yourself to a student you've never met before in your school.

Level 2 - Invite a student you've never talked to before to hangout with you and your friends

Level 3 - Meet 2 students you've never talked to before, invite the student to hang with you and your friends 3 days of this week, and find out 4 things you all have in common.

#NewFriend
#LiveIntentionally

Recipient of your Challenge:

Recipient's Reaction:

How did it make you feel?

Week 25

Intentionally Blackout

Level 1 & 2 - This week substitute your normal television and gamer time with reading a new book and try to complete it by the end of the week!

Level 3 - This week substitute your normal television and gamer time with reading a new book and try to complete it by the end of the week! Challenge yourself to go a full day without any social media.

#Blackout
#LiveIntentionally

Recipient of your Challenge:

Recipient's Reaction:

How did it make you feel?

Week 26

CONGRATULATIONS!!!

You made it through your challenge! Use this week to read through your logs. Your intentional acts of kindness have impacted the lives you intentionally set out to change. Please share your story on your social media. Use the hashtag, "#LiveIntentionally" and we'll find it.

Write me @ info@MrIntentional.com and let me know what you thought about your experience. Use the next page to log your FULL experience.

#LiveIntentionally

Join our *closed* Facebook community to share your experiences during this challenge:
www.facebook.com/groups/LiveIntentionally

Twitter: @MrBeIntentional
Periscope: @MrBeIntentional
Facebook: www.facebook.com/MrBeIntentional

Recipient of your Challenge:

Recipient's Reaction:

How did it make you feel?

About the Author

At the young age of 19, Mark Bush began his law enforcement career as a Correctional Officer with the Dallas County Sheriff's Department in Dallas, TX.   He quickly advanced to the position of Detention Training Officer before his 20th birthday. Shortly after Mark's 21st birthday, he made one of the best decisions of his life: he joined the United States Air Force.

While in the Air Force, Mark was able to continue his law enforcement career as a Security Force (Military Police) member. Within three months of getting to his first duty station, Mark deployed to Iraq, December 2004. Two years into his military career, Mark decided to work towards becoming a Military Working Dog Handler. After his hard work and dedication, Mark was selected to join the elite Military Working Dog Program.   As a Military Working Dog Handler, Mark deployed to Iraq in 2008 and 2009-2010 as an Explosive Detection Dog Handler.   January 5, 2010, Mark and his Military

Working Dog "Chukky", were credited with finding a Vehicle Borne Improvised Explosive Device (Car Bomb) with 50 lbs of homemade explosives also saving hundreds of lives. For his meritorious service while deployed to Iraq, The Secretary of the Army awarded Mark with the Army Commendation Medal.

As a handler, Mark was selected to support multiple United States Secret Service missions for; The President and Vice President of the United States, President of Russia, Chief of Staff of the Air Force, Director of the CIA, and Governor Arnold Schwarzenegger. Mark also spent a year of his career as an Air Force Investigator and Joint Drug Task Force Investigator Liaison to the Air Force Office of Special Investigations. Over the span of his eleven year career, Mark received multiple awards. Mark is most proud of his two Air Force Commendation Medals, an Army Commendation Medal, and his Veteran of the Month award from the Mayor of Rapid City, South Dakota.

Mark is currently the Director of Operations for Primecare Home Care Services, Inc. He oversees the day to day operations of four offices that provide expert in-home care solutions (RNs, LPNs, CNAs and PCAs) for seniors and individuals with developmental disabilities.

Mark is also the CEO/President of Saving Grace Security Solutions, LLC. While assigned to the United States Air Force Academy in Colorado Springs, CO from 2004 to 2007, Mark attended New Life Church in Colorado Springs. Mark was actively involved in small groups and the church choir. Shortly after Mark was transferred to Nevada in 2007, his Colorado church family experienced the devastating nightmare of an active shooter. Two members were killed and three were injured after a gunman opened fire as Sunday services were wrapping up.

Mark and his SGSS team tailored training specifically for church leaders based on their military and specialized training to mitigate the most loss of lives possible. Mark is determined to enhance the security mindset of church leaders and their staff to protect their flock.

Mark lives to inspire and impact the lives of the people around him. It's what gives him purpose in his own life.